"OK," NO IMMIGRATION REFORM

(BUT LET'S USE THE LAWS ALREADY ON THE BOOKS)

JBLAYNE JENNINGS

ISBN: 979-8-88640-262-9 (sc)
ISBN: 979-8-88640-263-6 (hc)
ISBN: 979-8-88640-264-3 (e)

One Galleria Blvd., Suite 1900, Metairie, LA 70001
1-888-421-2397

CONTENTS

INTRODUCTION

Millions of dollars are lost each year because no one seems to be paying attention to those persons in the United States without status or the illegal alien. Of course, there are many complaints, but there seems to be no effort to take advantage of the situation as it exists. In other words, what good can come from the present [perceived] dilemma? [1]

Great sums of money are lost, in that the illegal alien is not asked to pay "his fair share," due to mere presence in the United States. So then, this person drives on the highways, uses the health care services, is protected by the police and fire departments, his children "must" go to the public schools, etc. And for all of these benefits, the illegal alien is not asked to pay taxes and/or has no other responsibility to do anything whatsoever. It is now time for the illegal immigrant to pay his way in the United States. No pay, no benefits!

Moreover, this same individual is allowed to use the court systems. In criminal cases, he is provided counsel (if he cannot afford to pay for his own) at the government's expense (state and federal government); in civil cases, he may use an appointed government attorney, if he is unable to pay. And for these benefits, nothing is asked of the illegal alien. We ask nothing and he gives nothing. We don't want, expect, or allow him to work, so he cannot pay taxes. Well, America, you can't have it both ways! [2]

Nothing is asked of the illegal alien because most people only complain about the person being in the country, along with his family, thus sucking up all of the benefits. And yet, this same illegal alien is not permitted to work, for one thing, and pay his fair share of taxes, be they state or local. If we compute a bare minimum amount of taxes (a simple example) as $1,000 per year for one illegal alien, and we multiply that sum by 11,000,000 (a general figure often cited), the total taxes lost in one year would be $11,000,000,000?????????????????????????????????? That can't be right!!!!!!!!!!!!!!!!!!!!!!!!!!!!!!! [3]

Furthermore, if those 11,000,000 were permitted to work, and to pay for the "work permit" (cost of $460) each year, the funds lost to the federal government comes to $5,060,000,000 per year. This sum is multiplied by other family members in the household of the illegal alien who may be eligible to work. Consequently, trillions of dollars are being lost each year, while we only complain that the person is here and out of status. It seems that our resentment has blinded our common sense. Looking back over the last ten to fifteen years of complaining, and considering all of the benefits that the illegal alien has received (add into the mix the health care services from hospitals and health care facilities), the amounts lost would "blow one's mind."

Considering the foregoing, I am motivated to propose some remedies, rather than complain about the matter.

According to its web site, the United States Citizenship Services (USCIS) is a component of the United States Department of Homeland Security (DHS). This is the agency that carries out the administrative functions that were formerly carried out by the former United States Immigration and Naturalization Services (INS). The, current USCIS has as its stated policy to promote national security, to eliminate case backlog, and to improve customer services. [4]

Some of the specific responsibilities of USCIS are to process immigrant visas, naturalization petitions, and asylum and refugee applications. Further, the agency is involved in making adjudications performed at service centers, and managing all other immigration benefit functions. [5] The United States immigration courts and immigration judges, and the Board of Immigration Appeals, which hears appeals from the immigration courts, are part of the Executive Office for Immigration Review (EOIR) within the United States Department of Justice. (USCIS is part of the Department of Homeland Security).

As is quite apparent, the "responsibility" for immigration policies is well organized on paper. However, it will be clearly demonstrated in this presentation that organization, policies, rules, laws, etc., are not enough; as a matter of fact, if we had to grade the current USCIS, as well as the justice department, the grade would be "D"!

This presentation does not support or encourage more laws. Rather, it is an attempt to encourage the use of the many laws presently in place; and those laws, it is argued, will address most of the categories for aliens presently in the United States. It is time to apply what we have, and not continue making new laws that are never fully implemented.

This account is written, based on personal experiences—the writer has thirty years of immigration experiences—by one who has intimate knowledge of the laws and inner workings of the immigration services in the United States of America. [6]

SUMMARY HISTORICAL SKETCH

President Ronald Reagan was, perhaps, the first United States president to understand that something was lacking in our American immigration policy. If he were not the first to perceive the depth of the problem, he certainly was the first United States president to sign into law a comprehensive approach to the resolution of the problem. It was understood, by him, that a system that is open needed to have plans to monitor (unlike the national debt—until we implode—there is no plan to deal with it) the orderly progression of such a massive system. [7]

For Mr. Reagan and the framers of the proposed legislation, there needed to be a plan or program to reach all of the immigrants who could be aided (we speak primarily of normal, law-abiding persons). Otherwise, some would feel left out and feel forgotten or abandoned. So, then, the Immigration Reform and Control Act of 1986 was implemented, which allowed any certain immigrant (legal or illegal) an opportunity to file with the government any application for which they felt they were qualified to file. This process of filing acted to protect the person from being deported, if he/she filed by a specific date. [8]

This comprehensive plan, signed into law by President Reagan, was intended to reach millions of immigrants in the United States at the time. However, the effort fell short, since there were not immediate benefits, and due to a lack of participation on behalf of those present in the United States. To remedy this lack of participation or enthusiasm, the plan was subsequently amended, whereby, again, one could file anything for which he qualified. Of course, as before, one would have to wait until his program or application came to fruition. This effort was, in a word, excellent, in that one could be protected merely by filing some type of application. Years later, even now, some of the filings are now coming into the final stages.

This waiting, in my mind, was a flaw in the process. Many of the programs or applications offered no immediate relief to those applying. For example, a United States citizen could have sponsored his sibling; well, this was filed, but it could take ten or twelve years before a visa would become current so the beneficiary could reap any benefit. Or, one may have had a labor certification application; after processing and approval, and subsequent filings to obtain visa qualification, it could still take years before any benefit would be available. But the person was protected from deportation proceedings.

Even though there were not, in some instances, immediate benefits, the "reform" action has good points in that many of the policies from these laws are good and one may still follow through on what had been previously started. In most instances, there was a process to follow that may take years. The process was not a one-shot deal—that is to say, one does not file in one day, and reap benefits the next day or week or year. To receive anything, the process may need to run *its* course. It was understood that many of the affected persons did not apply, given the opportunity to do so, because many illegal aliens were—and still are—reluctant and apprehensive, and thus failed to take advantage of the opportunity. So, according to Examiner.com, this spurred another amnesty bill under President Bill Clinton in 1994, an amnesty for illegal aliens. (Section 245 (i) was added to the FY 1995 Commerce, Justice, State Appropriations Bill. This amnesty ended on September 30, 1997, and resulted in 578,000 illegal aliens being granted permanent legal status.) [9]

In addition, and still relying on Examiner. Com, President Bill Clinton was responsible for the following: The Nicaraguan Adjustment and Central American Relief Act (NACARA) Amnesty of 1997, which granted amnesty to 1,000,000 illegal aliens from Central America; The Haitian Refugee Immigration Fairness Act Amnesty (HRJFA) of 1998, which granted amnesty to 125,000 illegal aliens from Haiti. In 2000, amnesty was granted to around 400,000 illegal aliens who claimed that they should have been amnestied under the amnesty of 1986;

and the Legal Immigration Family Equity (LIFE) Act Amnesty of 2000 removed deportation orders and/or granted permanent legal residency to an estimated 900,000 illegals. In all, it is estimated that under President Bill Clinton, an additional 3,000,000 illegal aliens were granted assistance. [10]

And once again (where fear rules over reason), many have not applied under the reform policies. We still have millions who never filed anything, at all; those who did file something are fearful and have not taken any action. So, reform after reform after new reform and new laws after new laws do not seem to solve the problem. It is time to stop passing new laws!

The net result is that we have fear of, often coupled with intimidation by, the Department of Justice and the courts; plus, we have those who say that we want nothing done unless and until we make the necessary adjustments at the borders. As per an article in Wikipedia, the free encyclopedia, it was stated that the INS was widely seen as ineffective after the scandals that arose after September 11, 2001. President George V. Bush signed the Homeland Security Act of 2002 into law, thus effectuating major changes on the borders and within the core of the United States. [11]

A PROPOSED REMEDY FOR SOME ILLEGAL ALIENS

Several years ago, I was working in the Washington, DC metro area (DC, MD, and VA). At that time, there were several of my clients who qualified for immigration benefits under a certain provision of the law. However, there was one problem: these individuals were not scheduled to appear in immigration court. Without anything more, it appeared that there was nothing that could be done for these clients.

Deciding not to give up, I approached the local immigration officials to see if my clients could be processed for court and appear before an immigration judge. This approach worked, and several of these persons were able to take advantage of existing laws to obtain their permanent residency status.

Moving ahead to this present time, I recently approached local immigration officials in Florida and asked if my clients could be processed to take advantage of another provision of the law. As before, the client would have to be in deportation proceedings before he/she could take advantage of this provision of the law. Even though the clients were qualified in all respects (no criminal record, long presence in the United States, good character, etc.), I was informed that there was no longer "any" policy in place to accommodate persons who wanted to go to court to pursue relief available to them.

On June 10, 2009, it was reported by the Liberally Conservative (a social group) that United States President Obama had granted terrorists US Constitutional Rights. In this regard, they (terrorists) are required to be given the Miranda Warning; i.e. the right to remain silent, warned that anything said can be held against them, right to an attorney if one cannot be afforded, etc.). This means that the United States has extended constitutional protection to those who have vowed to kill every American, wherever found in the world, but a "mere" illegal immigrant who qualifies for benefits cannot get them because he has no way to be placed in deportation proceedings (cannot get to the courthouse) to assert his rights to support himself and his family. Wow!

Contrary to popular belief, benefits have been on the books for the illegal alien for many years before that "nasty little word," amnesty, was used. In this manner, the Supreme Court of the United States in 1950 (Johnson v. Eisentrager, 339 US 763,771) said: "In extending constitutional protection beyond the citizenry, the Court has been at pains to point out that it was the alien's presence within the territorial jurisdiction that gave the Judiciary power to act." In other words, if the alien is present in the United States, he has the protection of the US Constitution.

Before the case in 1950, the Supreme Court said as early as 1896 (citing a case from 1886) in Wong Wing v. US (183 US 228) that illegal aliens have protections under the Fourteenth Amendment to the US Constitution. It necessarily follows that illegal aliens cannot be deprived of life, liberty, or property without due process of law, and they are entitled to equal access to the courts, among other protections.

Previously, it was noted that certain benefits are available to the illegal immigrant, but that there was no way to assert those rights. Well, that is not the whole story. The rest of the story is that immigration services very often (almost always) will place illegal aliens into deportation (now called removal) proceedings when they are arrested and go to jail (on any charge): i.e. no driver's license, drunk driving, theft, etc. Considering this procedure (when an illegal alien is arrested), an immigration officer will visit the jails (daily) to determine if there are persons detained who are out of status or illegal. If so, the officer will place a detainer or hold on the illegal immigrant. This means that (by law) the illegal alien will have to be turned over to immigration when the criminal case is concluded.

When the criminal or traffic case is concluded (probation or serving time or disposition by some other means), the illegal alien is taken into custody by immigration officials and will face an immigration judge at some future date. Whereas there could be no bond when the illegal alien was, previously, in jail, and before the disposition of the criminal case, the illegal alien can now apply for a bond before the immigration judge. During the immigration proceedings, one can apply (now) for whatever relief that he/she is qualified to receive.

In a nutshell, then, immigration officers refuse to allow an illegal alien the opportunity to pursue benefits that are only available through the immigration court system only if an individual is arrested, has to go to jail, and cannot get a bond—requiring the facility detaining the illegal alien to feed and house him, unnecessarily, until immigration collects the person and detains him again, unless and until he gets a bond from the immigration court, or not. On the contrary, this same illegal alien cannot, cannot, cannot decide to pursue his/her rights voluntarily. Unless the time and money is "wasted" by the government (state and federal), and the alien is placed into deportation proceedings by immigration officials, he has no rights. One cannot agree to be placed into deportation proceedings and face being deported to go back to their country. So, the illegal alien cannot stay, and he can't go home! Does this make sense to anybody?????????????

Now, as stated, when I am asked by an illegal alien (illegal because of overstaying or having come into the country illegally) how to get immigration benefits that are available by existing laws in immigration court, my response is to advise the client that he/she could get arrested; that is to say, go out and commit a crime or a traffic offense. This present system has driven or encouraged an increase in criminal behavior in the United States—an absurd result driven by waste, insensitivity, and a misunderstanding of what is needed to address the problem of immigration in the United States.

The government should take a hard look at existing laws and procedures; and put into place reasonable steps that may be taken by the illegal alien when there is legal relief available, and not fight the alien at every turn. A person should be able to face deportation, if that is what he or she may desire. And lest we forget, the government should take care to insure that the public is not outraged to learn that there are trillions of dollars—each year— that are lost to the state and federal governments that could be paid for taxes and application fees alone.

Aside from the money that is lost by not following a proper procedure for illegal aliens who qualify for existing benefits, my most important point in this presentation is that these persons have constitutional rights that were recognized over one hundred years ago by the United States Supreme Court. To deny these rights is to deny the illegal alien the right to support himself, and his family; so, we do not need new laws or immigration reform to grant relief that is already available. Congress or the president does not need to act; let's enforce/implement the laws that are already on the books.

The USCIS is just an example of the typical federal agency. With that having been said, the general public, in America, does not have a good impression of this agency. More to the point, not only does the American public lack respect for this agency, the illegal alien (looking through his eyes) sees massive waste, corruption, gross incompetence, and profound intimidation of the immigrant community. Moreover, if a problem is to be solved using the "political" component of the government, few believe that there is any hope, whatsoever.

On the one hand, one may say that these governmental agencies need a face-lift; on the other hand, the truth is that this agency needs major surgery. In this vein, the perception needs to change, in that the mission of the agency needs to be understood, and confidence needs to be generated, thus carrying out its intended purpose, and not causing harm.

As an initial effort, our Department of Justice (as well as the USCIS) needs to review all laws, rules, regulations, and procedures that are outdated, antiquated, or that do not work; similarly, there needs to be a revision of these laws, rules, and procedures, where necessary. It necessarily follows that such laws, rules, etc., will need to be identified, thus determining the "true" purpose of such laws, rules, etc. If such a law or rule has lost its effect or meaning or purpose or is outdated, the question then becomes: can this rule be revised or saved so that it may have some practical effect? To demonstrate this point, consider an existing law or procedure of immigration whereby one who has been present in the United Sates since January 1972 may apply for his permanent status (green card), if there has been continual presence in the United States without interruption, no criminal record, and the applicant is of good moral character.

This procedure whereby one may apply for his permanent status (green card) if he has been present in the United States since 1972 is an excellent procedure, as are several other procedures presently in existence— except that it is "OUTDATED." In this regard, this law is more than twenty years old. When first enacted, a person needed twenty years to satisfy the requirements of this law— now one needs forty-two years to satisfy the same requirements. The net result is that there are thousands, or evens millions, of persons who could have or may satisfy the requirements of this procedure, if anyone had been paying attention. But this procedure requires legislative or governmental action (big problem). Is there any wonder why we have such a big "mess" in our immigration procedures?

It seems perfectly clear that competent persons are needed in key positions to seriously evaluate laws, rules, policies, and procedures. Further, it seems rather basic that laws should reflect the changing times. In other words, the laws should keep up with the times. On this note, an agency or the government must consider the changing times, and that actions taken years in the past need to be constantly reviewed to determine if anything else is needed. It is not prudent to forget past laws, for they may resolve many of the present and future problems. If a review is done on a regular basis, we may move forward and remain relevant and effective.

America is a great country—perhaps the greatest country ever to have existed. But there are those—in America—who would disagree. Nevertheless, one reason I feel that it is the greatest is because of the gathering of many peoples from all over the world. But because of the many freedoms and privileges that Americans have enjoyed, we have begun to take these freedoms and privileges for granted, thus having become, somewhat, complacent. Following this line of thinking, a typical routine is that one will rise early in the morning, go to work, return home and have dinner, and then go to bed—after a little TV. The next day, the same routine is followed. Now, if we ask ten Americans on the street to explain his/her purpose in life, only a few will have a response. We seem to have lost our way. Is there any wonder why Asians and others come to America and excel in math and science and begin businesses, while the "American" complains about someone taking his job???? They (the new foreigners) have a hunger for the things that we take for granted, and for what we have always had available to us.

Using the foregoing as a background, consider the notion that some workers will bring a "lackadaisical" attitude to the work place. Many of these individuals work for the federal government—we have recently seen the mess that we have with the Internal Revenue Service—and are charged with providing services to the public. But instead of services, we get persons in positions who consider themselves little "gods." Those persons only want to finish the day, going through the motions of working, and go home to watch more TV. There is no one to motivate these workers because the supervisors are in the same boat.

Taking a closer look at the federal governmental agencies involved, I have often wondered (during over thirty years of exposure) why immigration officials have such bad attitudes. This includes government attorneys in and out of court. It seems that everyone is always angry; they are rude and disrespectful to everyone. One would think that these government workers are not there to serve the public. Rather, they appear to be there to intimidate. No one seems to understand that such hostile actions cause the agency to suffer. It causes the agency to suffer when immigration officials raid one's home at 4 a.m. to arrest someone who is not in status, disturbing families with small children, with guns in hand; or, being known for raiding chicken factories, while known terrorists walk across the border unhampered. The immigration officials, perhaps, feel that an illegal immigrant working in a chicken factory is more dangerous than one who has vowed to kill every American. That seems to be the mindset.

And yet, there is a better way to resolve the great debate. The question becomes this: "What is to be done with the illegal alien with his wife and five children who have been here for years and contribute nothing to our way of life?" He has been here for years along with 11,000,000 more of his kind. They have sucked up benefits from health to schools, police and fire protection, and have dared to work, without permission. Is this illegal immigrant useless, or does he have any value whatsoever? I say, Yes!!!!!! And it is time for him (them) to start paying their way. No more free lunches. It's time to pay the piper. No more going without paying taxes, all taxes, state and local. This is a nation of laws and we all abide by the laws, and take responsibility for ourselves and our families. It's time to come out from the shadows.

With the "JBJ Plan," there is no need for new legislation. No one can say the magic word "AMNESTY" because of any new laws that will take effect. There is no need for the left to say give us this, or for the right to say we shall give nothing at all. There is no need for Congress to pass thousands of pages of laws (not yet read), and decide to read them or interpret them after everyone has voted on the laws, but not read or understood what is in the law. Instead, it is time to use and recognize the laws that have been already passed.

Let us suppose, for a minute, that the past legislators—being at least as intelligent as we are today—had a grasp for the problems of immigration during their time. They understood the problems at hand and devised a framework from which the present and future problem of immigration could be addressed. Contrary to their ideals, this present generation has chosen to ignore the structure and framework of past laws and has done nothing to update or revise procedures and laws to comport with the times. If this had been done, we would have been able to address new arrivals, deal with the existing populace, and address what should be done at the borders. Has everyone been asleep?

The "JBJ Plan" embraces the concept of bringing about immediate results, based on existing laws (when used, including rules, regulations, and procedures). With that predicate in mind, there are several existing laws that will accommodate millions—yes millions—of illegal aliens that are in the United States, without passing any new laws or without any executive orders from the president of the United States. Some of these laws are being used (partially), while others (laws) are not being used at all. And the funny thing is, not ha ha funny—no one seems to really care. At the same time, there are other laws that are being misused.

As an example of laws not being used, I previously mentioned, herein, the outdated law whereby one who had been present in the United States since January 1,

1972, could apply for his/her permanent status. Of course, this person must not have any significant criminal record, and must have complied with all laws while present in the United States. This person could not have paid taxes, because he/she would not have been able to work (and yet, some illegal aliens do work and pay taxes using a temporary social security number). This person also must be a person of good moral character.

When this law was passed, it is certain that the framers decided what the important qualifications were, and did not extend this provision of the law to criminals or to persons who did not have good moral character. In spite of the care in passing such a provision, and the implementation of it, it is rarely used today. Why? It is rarely used because not too many people know about it, and it has not been revised over the years. In this regard, when the law was passed, a person could take advantage of this provision if he/she had been present in the United States for twenty years. Today, in order for one to take advantage of this provision, he/she would have had to be present for forty-two years. The years have more than doubled because no one is paying attention to the laws and the requirements.

Equally so, no one is paying attention to the trillions of dollars that this nation could take advantage of, if anyone cared. Where are those organizations that (supposedly) espouse the rights of the illegal alien? Where are the advocates who say that they are for the rights of all? Don't they know about the United States Supreme Court cases that give constitutional rights to the illegal alien? Where are the senators, the congressmen, congresswomen—many of whom are lawyers—to stand for the rights of the illegal alien, thus pointing out that there are laws existing to grant immediate assistance to the illegal immigrant.

So, with this law for persons who have been here since 1972, is it now time to revise this law and make it practical, consistent with the intent of the original legislators? If this would be done, thousands, if not millions, of illegal aliens would be helped.

Under the present law, the common belief is that one who came into the United States illegally has no relief. This notion has also been extended to persons who have overstayed for certain periods of time. Contrary to popular belief, there is relief (help) available to one who has a citizen spouse (husband or wife) and came into the United States illegally and/or has overstayed. The popular belief is that everyone has to depart the United States, go back to their home country, and go through the United States Embassy after obtaining a waiver.

The truth is that there are two procedures. Using the first procedure, if one decides that he/she wants to go through the United States Embassy in their home country, that person will have to get a visa. To do this, if one is married to a United States citizen, the citizen may sponsor the spouse; after approval of the sponsorship, that beneficiary files his/her application for a visa. During the interim, the beneficiary of the citizen spouse may file (this is a new procedure) for a waiver to show extreme hardship of the citizen wife (to include permanent resident or citizen children and parents). If the waiver is approved, the beneficiary is scheduled for an interview at the United States Embassy. If successful at the interview, that person may return to the United States as a permanent resident.

This is not a desired procedure, because many illegal aliens do not want to leave the United States. They do not want to take the chance of not being able to return. So, this procedure, even though available, is not often used—except when a person has been deported, and has to leave, this is the procedure that is to be used, whereby one may apply for a visa through the United States embassy. The person seeking this type of visa is required to also show that he/she has a good record or no significant criminal record, and is, of course, of good moral character.

Let us digress for a moment and consider the following fictional scenario in asserting what is expected from our United States Congress: John, while visiting Washington, DC, a few months in the past, had the fortune—or misfortune—of meeting and having a conversation with Harry, who just so happens to be a member of the United States Congress. Harry immediately informed John that he (Harry) was a very important and powerful man. John was informed that Harry had the power to determine what bills/legislation would be passed or not; and that—in a word—his power was "absolute."

John's interest being aroused, he asked Harry, a most powerful person, why Congress refused to act on very important issues, such as balancing the budget, national security, social security, problems with the Veterans Administration, and immigration, to name a few. Harry responded to John by saying: "Son, did I tell you that I am a very important person? And to answer your question in summary, let me say that most people in America do not understand that the most important function of Congress is to "preserve the institution, for everything else is secondary."

John, not understanding this answer, pressed further. Harry went on to explain—after being ensured that his comments were off the record—that the congressional system, being rooted and grounded in nepotism and cronyism, was designed or has devolved into a system whereby consistency and longevity is the rule. Following this point, it was stated that "nothing" is more important than keeping a congressional member in place; in this way, there must be consistency for a solid basis to propose and pass desired legislation. But first, the donor or contributor—that person who gives the money—must be recognized and pampered. Pampered, in that he/she must be able to get what he/she wants or expects for the money that has been given. This keeps the money coming.

Harry explained (using a real example) that some donor may want a grant to study why birds seem to have synchronized movement while in flight (that is to say, they can all turn at the same moment, as if the movements are being communicated to them). This grant costs the taxpayers $15,000,000. Going further, Harry told of another grant, whereby one donor felt that he needed $40,000,000 to show that monkey urine, when mixed with aspirin, might be a cure for cancer. It was emphasized that while these causes may seem trivial to the average person, the reverse is true, because donors needed to be shown preference to keep the money coming (preserving the institution)!

While referring to another member of congress, Harry exclaimed that Nancy hit the "nail on the head" when she said (while justifying a proposed, and passed, very important piece of legislation—but she had not read the bill) that we have not read this several-thousand-page bill because we have not had time, but we needed to get it passed; since it was now passed and was law, we can all read it and see what was in it. Really???

Turning back to more serious and factual matters, consider the second procedure that is existing law and whereby an illegal alien who is married to a United States citizen, and does not want to go home. This person may be sponsored by the citizen spouse (or permanent resident) but has to wait until the visa number becomes current; when the application for sponsorship has been approved, the illegal alien may file for his/her permanent residency, or green card. And in spite of laws that specifically provide the benefits to qualified persons, great, great, great confusion exists in the workplace.

Immigration officials in the state of North Carolina had problems with this provision of the law—only after first denying the benefits were the benefits granted, based on an appeal from the local field office. Recently in Florida, courts and immigration officials have shown that they still do not get it. It is clear that the law states that one who is in the United States illegally or came in illegally may apply for permanent residency (green card) contemporaneous with filing the appropriate waiver. (The law was given to them in their hands).

To qualify for this procedure, one must be married to a United States citizen (or permanent resident), must not, must not have any significant criminal record, be of good moral character, and the citizen spouse and/or citizen or permanent resident children or parent(s) must experience extreme hardship, if the applicant would be deported from the United States.

Still, not willing to read, understand, and implement the laws, there have been immigration officers, immigration judges, and immigration attorneys who have said to my clients that they would have to leave the United States if they plan to get their permanent residency or green card. Because of this confusion that persists, most of the persons who qualify for these benefits (the illegal-alien community) are fearful and will not apply for the benefits for which they qualify.

As an aside, let me point out that the composition of illegal immigrants in the United States is more than Mexican. There are illegal immigrants from Asia, Africa, Europe, South America, Central America, etc. These aliens may have come into the United States illegally, while others may have come in legally and overstayed, i.e. students, visitors, investors, etc. Mexicans make up a small portion of the illegal alien community. So, we don't have to beat up the Mexicans. [12]

America needs to understand that (right now, today) there are laws on the books that address [nearly] every category of illegal alien. There is the provision that addresses persons who have been in the United States for many years (registry provision—this provision needs to be revised); there is the provision that addresses persons who have been here for ten years or more with family (extreme requirements need to be lifted); there is a provision for persons who marry United States citizens or permanent residents and do not have to leave the country; there are several procedures for persons who are in immigration court proceedings; there are provisions for children who are wards of the state; and there are provisions for persons who have committed crimes (not discussed herein).

CONCLUSION

Our message, in sum, is that immigration reform is not an answer or the answer. We should assume that our forebears were "at least" as intelligent as we are. Let's look at what has already been done and expand on it to see if the answers are right before us. Don't look at the trees—see the whole forest. Start with public awareness of the services that already exist for most of the population in question. Whether there are seminars, public meetings, advertising, or some other means, awareness is the "key." The remedy is not or should not be left up to new laws (which will bring about, in some instances, redundancy), but in the application of what we already have. Let us see the forest, but remember there are also trees that make up the forest.

My plan, then, does not ask the Democrats, or Republicans, or the Green Party, or Tea Party, or Independents to do anything except to look at (collectively) what we already have, and to move forward.

NOTES

1. In 2013, a DHS report estimating the size of the illegal immigrant population in the US as being 11.4 million in 2012 compared to 11.5 in January of 2011(Wikipedia, the free encyclopedia).

2. Unlike most other federal agencies, USCIS is funded almost entirely by user fees. See USCIS official website.

3. An example as to the cost of operations may be gleamed from the budget request of President George W. Bush for FY2008. He received about 1 % from congressional appropriations and about 99% coming from fees~ the USCIS budget for that year was $2.6 billion (USCIS FY2008 fact sheet).

4. See official website (http://I.:"\'l-w.uscis.gov).

5. See USCIS Official website.

6. J. Blayne Jennings, the author, is a private citizen who has been a trial attorney for forty years. Thirty of those years involved practicing immigration law.

7. The Immigration Reform and Control Act of 1986 (IRCA), Pub.L.99-603, enacted Nov. 6, 1986, also known as the Simpson-Mazzoli Act, and was signed into law by President Ronald Reagan. This was an act of Congress that reformed immigration law.

8. In an article by Wikipedia (Immigration Reform and Control Act of 1986), the INS, now USCIS, estimated that about four million illegal immigrants would apply for legal status through the act and that roughly half of them would be eligible.

9. See www.examiner.comarticle/did-you-knowpresident-granted-amnesty-to-millions-of-illegal-aliens.

10. Examiner.com.

11. Homeland Security Act of 2002. Special report (http://www.usdojloig/special/0205/full report. pdf), May 20, 2002, www.usdoj.gov.

12. The Center for Immigration Services, as well as the Pew Hispanic Center and others keep track of illegal immigrants.

www.ingramcontent.com/pod-product-compliance
Lightning Source LLC
Chambersburg PA
CBHW020945160726
47993CB00007B/2952